of Heaven

PATRICIA O'TOOLE

Inspirational messages from the angels

Vol 1

blackbird

Copyright © Patricia O'Toole 2019

Published by Blackbird Digital Books

www.blackbird-books.com

A CIP catalogue record for this book is available from the British Library

ISBN 9781916426849

Original cover artwork © Josephine Wall. Used under licence. Licensed from Entertainment One Licensing US, Inc

The moral right of the author has been asserted.

Interior Images c. Olga Korneeva, Shutterstock

To my two sons, without whom none of this would have seemed possible

A Little Piece of Heaven contains channelled messages from the angels.

They were recorded over the seven-year period from 2004 to 2011, when my ability to communicate with angelic beings first began, and offer a fascinating glimpse into a celestial world. A world filled with love, stunning beauty and vibrant technicolour. All of the messages are very beautiful, simple to understand and easy to live by and I know that the angels would love you to incorporate them into your daily lives.

I hope that you enjoy using them as much I have enjoyed receiving them from the angels and that they may come to be a source of great comfort to you.

Patricia

Introduction

I never expected to be someone who would be able to see angels. I knew so little of them, other than what I had learnt in school or from going to church every Sunday as a child. I didn't know of anyone who could communicate with angelic beings and I doubt that I would have believed this was possible. In fact if someone had told me they could, I would probably have given them an extremely wide berth.

Yet, it seems that the angels had different ideas and were already working behind the scenes on this matter, when one crisp autumn evening an angel appeared completely unexpectedly before me; shimmering in the most beautiful shade of indigo blue that I had ever seen. It completely took my breath away and no matter how I look at it, my life has never been the same since.

At the time of the angels' arrival I was neither overly religious nor sceptical of faith, and living deep in the heart of the Irish countryside with my two sons. Our home, an old farmhouse set deep in a valley close to a long meandering river, was nothing out of the ordinary, yet it was here that the angels first appeared.

No-one could have predicted the events of that first night. It was a perfectly normal evening and I had just arrived home from work. Switching off the car engine after a 45-minute commute from the city, the silence of the countryside swept in around me like a soft blanket. As I fumbled my way through the darkness towards the front door, for some reason I hesitated, pausing to look up into the vast night sky. Hundreds of stars gazed back at me, set apart like sparkling diamonds in the endless expanse and I couldn't help but admire their beauty. I stood watching them for several minutes, until the chill of the night air sent me in search of the warmth of the house. Had I sensed something was about to happen? I will never know for sure, but on opening the front door, there was nothing out of the ordinary to greet me. Thomas, my youngest son was settled down to his homework in the sitting room, while Lee, my eldest son, had already sailed away on his bicycle to his evening job at a local restaurant. Everything was in its place. All was as it should be.

Thomas and myself had been home together for about an hour or so, when seemingly out of nowhere, the angel appeared before us. I recognised it instantly as an angelic being because it was so similar to that of those I had seen depicted on stained glass windows in church. I was completely taken aback. It hadn't flown in, walked by, floated down or swept past us. It just simply appeared and was gazing at Thomas, who was obviously able to see it too, as he was quietly looking back. A feeling of panic began to take over my initial shock which was fading fast, but as it did, I received a telepathic message telling me not to be afraid, as it was Archangel Michael. And just like the appearance of an angel, the message seemed to come from absolutely nowhere. My panic turned to disbelief. How could this be possible? I turned to Thomas, whispering across what I could see and hear and was further dumbfounded when he told me he already knew, as he too had heard the message and could see Archangel Michael clearly.

Realising we were sharing the same incredible phenomena has to be one of the most amazing experiences of my whole life. The room began to fill with an energy that I did not recognise and a deep sense of peace settled around us. It was unbelievably beautiful. It felt as though we had entered some kind of sacred sanctuary, even though neither of us had moved and nothing about the house had changed, other than the angel's appearance.

Suddenly I was overwhelmed by a feeling of being loved. It washed over me in waves and was so unexpected and intense that it completely took my breath away, bringing tears to my eyes. Then there was a sensation of being held and I realised that I had become enfolded within enormous wings. The feeling is difficult to explain other than to say it was not of this earth and it was this sensation that became my way of knowing whenever angels were near.

After this first startling encounter, it didn't take too long before many other angels began to visit us regularly. They also began to appear to my eldest son Lee. He too was completely taken aback by what was happening. It was irrelevant where we were going, what we were doing, or even whether we were together or not, when angels would silently appear. No-one else was able to see what we could and we quickly learnt to stay silent on the subject in the company of others.

Yet, once we were alone together at home we learnt a great deal about angels. At first they simply gazed at us silently, drifting in and out of focus. After much reading up on the subject, we realised that Thomas was able to see them clearly as a clairvoyant, while I could see them through my third eye and Lee could feel their presence as a clairsentient. As we were adjusting to this unusual information, the angels then began to communicate with us and we discovered that we were all clairaudient. We had the ability to hear voices from another realm – as I described in my first book *Call of an Angel*.

Speaking for myself, becoming familiar with being clairaudient certainly didn't happen overnight, but I found that if I sat quietly and 'listened' in a way that I had never done before, I clearly heard words and phrases when the angels were present. They never exactly struck up a conversation, but communicated using short simple phrases and their words were very easy to decipher from my own thoughts as they were so different to how I think and feel.

I soon realised that there was one major problem with this method of communication because as soon as I heard a message, it would immediately leave my mind and no matter how hard I tried to recall it, it was gone. This became quite frustrating as the messages were all so beautiful. I started to try to jot them down as soon as I heard them. Whether it was on a piece of paper, as a text on my phone, or on the back of my hand, it didn't really matter as long as I wrote them down before they were forgotten. However I soon realised that this was not always possible or practical, especially when I was at work. I attempted noting them down in some kind of code so that no-one would understand what I had written, but then I often didn't understand them either, and unfortunately some of the messages are lost forever; but many were not, and I soon began to compile them in a small notebook at home.

I wasn't sure what I was going to do with them all, but each one was carefully logged into my book, alongside the date that it had been received. As the years swept by, my collection turned into quite a volume, until it felt as though receiving messages from the angels was as natural as breathing.

How to Use this Book

Find a few quiet moments in your day when you can spend some time alone with this book. You don't need to be in any particular place. You could be sat in bed in the morning, on a park bench in your lunch hour, or even on an evening commute. In other words, there is no such thing as the wrong time or place to connect with the angels.

While holding the book between your hands, bring your focus to your breathing, so that you become aware of your presence and place within the world around you. This is called grounding.

Remembering to stay focused on your breath, ask the angels to surround you in pure white light. You can do this either out loud or in your mind, whichever you feel comfortable with. You may sense a feeling of calm and peace settle all around you as the angels move in closer to you.

This is a beautiful feeling and you should try to let yourself relax into the moment. Within this quiet energy, ask the angels to guide you to a message in the book that they would like you to read today. Mentally take note of anything you feel, see or hear as the angels try to communicate with you at this time.

After a few moments, bring your attention back to the book in your hands. Open the book at any page you feel guided to look at. You may find that your finger or thumb is already in a certain place. If so, open the book there and read the channelled message on the page. If not, flick through the pages until you feel guided to stop.

Please remember that there is no right or wrong way to choose a message and that you will find a way that suits you best.

Read the message on the page. Does it seem relevant to your life right now? Even if it doesn't, don't dismiss it and don't be disappointed! The angels know exactly what we need in our lives at any given time, but can only guide us in the right direction if we are willing to follow through on their advice.

Pick up a pen or pencil and, on the blank page facing the channelled message, write down or draw any thoughts or feelings that come up for you about the message that the angels guided you to. You could also make a note of the date. As you continue to practice connecting with the angels in this way, you should find that you gain clarity in many areas of your life.

Good luck!

Messages from the Angels

Thank you for
your continued
Support

lots of love
from
Becca,
Jessica
+
Emily

*Each moment has its
own quiet miracles*

FOR YOUR THOUGHTS

*There is only one
true heartbeat, that
of nature. For
without it, nothing
else exists*

FOR YOUR THOUGHTS

*Take the path that
sets your soul
on fire*

FOR YOUR THOUGHTS

Beauty isn't out of a bottle. It's who you are

FOR YOUR THOUGHTS

When you let nature thrive, all sorts of magic begins to happen

FOR YOUR THOUGHTS

Who says you can't stop the clock? Try, by enjoying the moment you are in

FOR YOUR THOUGHTS

*What defines you is
what you hold dear
in your heart*

FOR YOUR THOUGHTS

Inner beauty is a catchphrase for something that already exists

FOR YOUR THOUGHTS

Life is the only journey where there is no going back

FOR YOUR THOUGHTS

Being sad is as important as being happy. Otherwise you will never fully understand either of them

FOR YOUR THOUGHTS

Time spent with nature is never lost

FOR YOUR THOUGHTS

If you let it, each day can be a new adventure

FOR YOUR THOUGHTS

*Stay grounded in this
lifetime and
everything will pass
in fleeting moments*

FOR YOUR THOUGHTS

When was it that we began to distance ourselves from the beautiful world around us?

FOR YOUR THOUGHTS

Shine your light brightly

FOR YOUR THOUGHTS

*There is no moment
like this moment, if it
is filled with love*

FOR YOUR THOUGHTS

*When you strip
everything back, isn't
it fabulous just to be
alive!*

FOR YOUR THOUGHTS

When you believe in yourself, anything is possible. It is that simple

FOR YOUR THOUGHTS

Be yourself, you are
only answerable to
your own heart and
it knows the way

FOR YOUR THOUGHTS

Very few people can say they have not loved. We were born to love, and to be loved

FOR YOUR THOUGHTS

Always remember to love yourself. It isn't a selfish notion. You will never be free of human conditioning if you don't

FOR YOUR THOUGHTS

A reflection in the river is not distorted. It is exactly what you are – perfect

FOR YOUR THOUGHTS

Heaven is way
nearer than you
think

FOR YOUR THOUGHTS

*The unspoken
language of the
universe is limitless*

FOR YOUR THOUGHTS

Let each thought be filled with love

FOR YOUR THOUGHTS

*Your inner
sanctuary is
always waiting
for you to come
and visit*

FOR YOUR THOUGHTS

Nature is always on our side

FOR YOUR THOUGHTS

*A kiss from the
sun is priceless*

FOR YOUR THOUGHTS

Each path is unique as we head towards the same destination

FOR YOUR THOUGHTS

*There are no weeds
in my garden, only
friends I have yet to
meet*

FOR YOUR THOUGHTS

Surround
yourself with
love

FOR YOUR THOUGHTS

Let go of pain
from your past
so that your soul
is free to
wander into
new beginnings

FOR YOUR THOUGHTS

*Angels always have
your back*

FOR YOUR THOUGHTS

Shower your world
with kindness and
leave the rest to fate

FOR YOUR THOUGHTS

*Your world is created
by what you put
into it*

FOR YOUR THOUGHTS

*You are never alone,
not even in your
darkest moments*

FOR YOUR THOUGHTS

The eye of a storm is usually the calmest moment. Perhaps before it even began

FOR YOUR THOUGHTS

There is one feeling
every sentient being
can recognise. The
vibration that comes
from love

FOR YOUR THOUGHTS

Remember when you thought the world was a magical place filled with wonder? It still is that same place, you have just forgotten your place within the magic

FOR YOUR THOUGHTS

Today, just be

FOR YOUR THOUGHTS

Thank you for every clean breath of air I take that you make

FOR YOUR THOUGHTS

*There is only one sort
of kindness and it
encompasses
everything*

FOR YOUR THOUGHTS

What do you see when you look at a wild flower? I see perfection

FOR YOUR THOUGHTS

When you fall in
love, know only
sweetness together

FOR YOUR THOUGHTS

*Nature has
perfection down
to a tee*

FOR YOUR THOUGHTS

*There is no need to
find another when
love finds your heart*

FOR YOUR THOUGHTS

Being aware is music
to the soul

FOR YOUR THOUGHTS

The quiet voice of nature can speak volumes without saying a word

FOR YOUR THOUGHTS

Show kindness in all you do

FOR YOUR THOUGHTS

~ Love ~
No Judgements
No Expectations
No Demands
Only Acceptance

FOR YOUR THOUGHTS

*It doesn't take much
to make a difference*

FOR YOUR THOUGHTS

All life matters

FOR YOUR THOUGHTS

Welcome to the world of angels

FOR YOUR THOUGHTS

Why are so many people living in the past or the future? Be alive today. Do your best today. And above all else, do no harm to any sentient being today

FOR YOUR THOUGHTS

*Be kind to all
living things*

FOR YOUR THOUGHTS

Each moment has its own quiet miracles

FOR YOUR THOUGHTS

Stay exactly as you are because there is no-one else like you. Therefore you are perfect

FOR YOUR THOUGHTS

Music frees the soul
from human
conditioning that
cannot be expressed
in words

FOR YOUR THOUGHTS

If the concept of being in the now continues to elude you, watch any flower, it has it down to perfection

FOR YOUR THOUGHTS

*Nature has an
uncanny way of
getting into your
every heartbeat*

FOR YOUR THOUGHTS

If you go to bed each night with a light heart you will understand paradise. When you don't, then seek it

FOR YOUR THOUGHTS

*Once upon a time
there was no need to
meditate because
peace and magic was
everywhere*

FOR YOUR THOUGHTS

Falling in Love with Nature

I received many of the messages in this book while I was outside walking in nature and because of this, I became much more aware of the natural beauty around me. Simple things such as the birds singing, or the rustle of the leaves in the breeze; the warmth from the sun, the stillness of a night sky and the beauty and delicacy of all living things.

What has become strikingly obvious, is how relevant many of the messages are now as we clamour to reverse climate change and preserve what remains of the natural world. Did the angels know that *A Little Piece of Heaven* could contribute a timely reminder from the celestial world for us to respect all life, no matter how small or insignificant it may seem? I like to think so, as one thing I have learnt from my association with the angelic world, is that nothing is ever by chance. Somehow, even though it may not always seem that way, everything is meant to be.

Patricia

A note from the publisher

If you would like to keep up with news of
Patricia and her books, including the
forthcoming Volume II of *A Little Piece Of
Heaven,* please sign up to our Patricia O'Toole
mailing list (securely managed by Mailchimp):
http://eepurl.com/c56Qy1

You can also connect with Patricia on Facebook
at her *Call of an Angel* Facebook page
https://www.facebook.com/callofanangel/

Also by Patricia O'Toole

What would you do if angels suddenly appeared in your life? Would you tell your family, friends & work colleagues? Or keep it a secret? Patricia O'Toole and her two teenage sons were living quietly in a remote corner of Ireland when one day, unexpectedly, everything changed. It all began when Patricia came across a long forgotten, soon-to-expire, gift voucher at the bottom of a drawer and decided to use it to visit a psychic. This decision led the whole family on an unexpected voyage of self-discovery when they realised that they all had an ability to both see, and communicate with, angels and spirits. True story of how extraordinary encounters with angels changed the lives of an ordinary working mum and her family forever.

Paperback/Large Print/Ebook

Call of an Angel by Patricia O'Toole - order online & from all good bookshops worldwide quoting ISBN number 9780995473584

The #authorpower publishing company
Discovering outstanding authors
www.blackbird-books.com
2/25 Earls Terrace, London W8 6LP
@Blackbird_Bks

blackbird
blic ble Publishers

Printed in Great Britain
by Amazon